WEST ELE...
1322 CENTRAL
STOUGHTON, MA 02072

W9-BRX-190

Welcome to China

Meredith Costain   Paul Collins

This edition first published in 2002 in the United States of America by Chelsea House Publishers, a subsidiary of Haights Cross Communications

All rights reserved. No part of this publication may be reproduced or transmitted in any form or by any means without the written permission of the publisher.

Chelsea House Publishers
1974 Sproul Road, Suite 400
Broomall, PA 19008–0914

The Chelsea House world wide web address is www.chelseahouse.com

Library of Congress Cataloging-in-Publication Data Applied for.
ISBN 0-7910-6548-0

First published in 2000 by
Macmillan Education Australia Pty Ltd
627 Chapel Street, South Yarra, Australia, 3141

Copyright © Meredith Costain and Paul Collins 2000

Edited by Miriana Dasovic
Text design by Goanna Graphics (Vic) Pty Ltd
Page layout by Goanna Graphics (Vic) Pty Ltd
Cover design by Goanna Graphics (Vic) Pty Ltd

Printed in Hong Kong

Acknowledgements
The author and the publisher are grateful to the following for permission to reproduce copyright material:

Cover photograph: Market scene in Guangxi Province, © Pelusey Photography.

All internal photographs by Pelusey Photography.

While every care has been taken to trace and acknowledge copyright the publishers tender their apologies for any accidental infringement where copyright has proved untraceable.

Contents

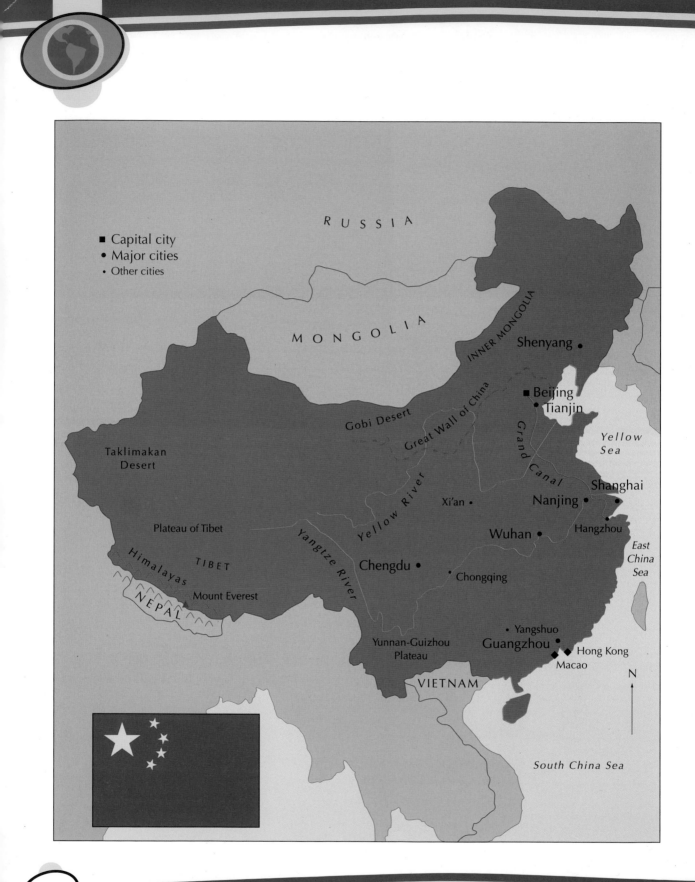

Capital city
Major cities
Other cities

RUSSIA

MONGOLIA

INNER MONGOLIA

Shenyang

Beijing
Tianjin

Yellow
Sea

Gobi Desert

Great Wall of China

Grand Canal

Taklimakan
Desert

Yellow River

Shanghai

Xi'an

Nanjing

Plateau of Tibet

Hangzhou

Yangtze River

Wuhan

East
China
Sea

Himalayas

TIBET

Chengdu

NEPAL

Mount Everest

Chongqing

Yunnan-Guizhou
Plateau

Yangshuo

Guangzhou

Hong Kong

Macao

VIETNAM

N

South China Sea

Welcome to China!

Hi!

Ni hao! My name is Mei Ling. I live in a village near Yangshuo, in the southern Chinese **province** of Guangxi.

China is huge. It is the third-largest country in the world, after Russia and Canada. It stretches all the way from Tibet in the west to the East China Sea in the east, and from the Mongolian border in the north to the border with Vietnam in the south.

China is a **communist** country. Its official name is the People's Republic of China. But my ancestors used to call their country Zhongguo, which means 'Middle Kingdom'. They chose this name because they thought their country was the center of the world.

There are more people living in China than in any other country. We have 56 different nationalities, including Mongol, Tibetan and Uighur. Most of the people are Han Chinese, like me. The people from the 55 **minority groups** mainly live in the border regions.

Many of the people from the minority groups, such as this Tibetan woman, still wear traditional costumes.

Family life

Although China is becoming more **industrialized**, many people still work on farms. My father, Huang, grows rice in the **rice paddies** that surround our village. He also grows vegetables in our garden.

My mother, Li, has her own business. She takes tourists on bicycle tours of the local area. The hills around my village have been sculpted by wind and water into strange shapes. They have funny names, which in English mean things such as Crab Hill, Green Frog Watching, and Enjoying the Moon.

I do not have any brothers or sisters. There are already more than one billion people in China, so government officials worry that there will not be enough food or land for everyone if the population continues to grow. Families are encouraged to have only one child. If people decide to have more children, they are fined, and lose some rights and benefits.

My grandmother, whom I call Nai Nai, lives with us. Chinese people respect and honor their elders. We believe it is our duty to care for our parents when they are too old to look after themselves.

The houses in our village are very simple. We do not have electricity or running water. We cook our meals on an open fire, and get our water from the local well.

School

Children start school in China at the age of seven. After six years of primary school we move up to secondary school. Some children in country areas are allowed to leave school early so they can help their parents in the fields. Other students go on to university to train to be doctors, engineers, scientists or teachers.

Our school day starts at 8:30 a.m. We have a 2-hour break for lunch, which gives me enough time to go home. After lunch we have more lessons and help the teacher by doing jobs around the school. The school day ends at 4:30 p.m. Many children who live in cities then go to a special activity center called a 'Children's Palace'. There they sing, draw pictures, make models with clay and do gymnastics and dancing.

I wish I could go to one of these places, too! Instead, I help my father in the garden.

Chinese children go to school every day except Sunday. Friday is a special excursion day in many schools. These children from Chengdu are on an art excursion.

We start each school day with 10 minutes of physical education. At primary school we learn to read and write a type of Chinese called Mandarin. We also study maths, history, geography, crafts and moral character. My favorite subject is art.

Sports and leisure

In China, people work very hard. There is not much time left in the day for leisure activities. But Chinese people think it is very important to stay fit. We exercise before we go to school or work. Some people gather in large groups before work to do slow, graceful movements called **tai ji quan**, or **tai chi**. Other people perform martial arts such as **gongu**, or **kung fu**. Chinese gymnasts often perform well at the Olympic Games.

Other popular sports are kite-flying, badminton, basketball and ping pong. So many people play ping pong that we think of it as our national sport. If people don't have a proper ping pong table, they make one by placing a table top on bricks. Even the net is made of bricks!

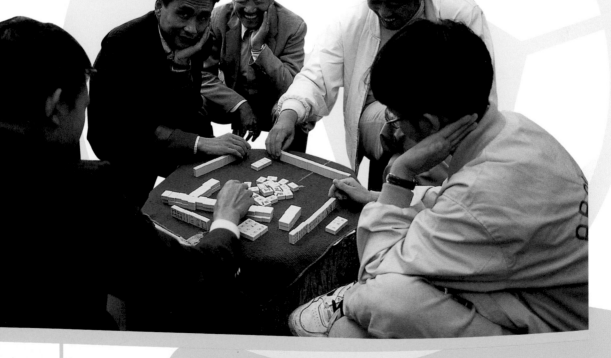

*In the evenings, people often get together to play games such as cards, Chinese chess or **mah jong**.*

Chinese culture

From the earliest times, Chinese craftspeople have made fine artwork such as paintings, calligraphy, sculpture, buildings and pottery. Many Chinese works of art feature landscapes, birds and flowers, showing the beauty of nature. They are painted on fans, screens and long panels, and are made of paper or silk.

Chinese Opera

Each region of China has its own traditional style of opera. The stories told are based on old legends and events from history. There is always a lot of loud singing, funny scenes, graceful dancing and skillful acrobatics.

Calligraphy

Earth

Water

Field

Chinese people use a brush and ink for their fine writing, called **calligraphy**. In the Mandarin language there are over 50,000 symbols, called characters. Each one is a little picture that stands for an object or an idea. Even though there are so many different characters, most people only know about 5,000. We learn 400 to 500 new characters each year at school.

Many people in China love going to the opera. The actors and singers in Chinese opera wear brightly colored costumes and heavy make-up.

In ancient times, calligraphy was thought to be the most beautiful of all the arts.

The Buried Soldiers of Xi'an

In 1974, some farm workers digging a well in Xi'an found buried treasure! Thousands of years ago, it was the custom to bury a king with his servants and warriors, so that they could protect him in the afterlife. But in this case, the 7,000 warriors found in the tomb were not real people. They were made of terracotta, a type of clay. Weapons, chariots and horses made of bronze were found in the pits beside the warriors.

The terracotta warriors of Xi'an were found in the tomb of the first emperor of China, Qin Shihuang. Each soldier has a slightly different face, making it look incredibly lifelike.

The symbol of the dragon is important in Chinese culture. It stands for fire, strength and activity. Dragons are often carved into or painted on the walls and roof supports of buildings. They are supposed to bring good fortune and long life to the people living there.

Festivals and religion

I always look forward to the first new moon of the new year, when we celebrate Spring Festival. We hang lucky red paper decorations around the house, and visit friends and relations. On New Year's Eve we stay up very late, talking and playing games. The next day, we go out onto the streets and celebrate. We also let off fireworks to scare away evil spirits. Two weeks later, when the moon is full, we celebrate the Lantern Festival. We walk through the streets at night, carrying glowing red lanterns shaped like goldfish and birds.

In the fifth lunar month, Chinese people celebrate the Dragon Boat Festival. We row dragon boats on our local rivers to honor the ancient poet Qu Yan. In mid-autumn, my family sits under the bright light of the full moon. We eat moon cakes, filled with lotus seeds or sweet red bean paste.

Chinese Festivals

Spring Festival	First new moon in January
Lantern Festival	First full moon after Spring Festival
Pure Brightness Day	April 5
Water-splashing Festival	April 13–15
Chinese Youth Day	May 4
Dragon Boat Festival	Fifth day of fifth lunar month
Children's Day	June 1
Ghost Month	Late August to late September
Teacher's Day	September 10
China's National Day	October 1

Festivals are colorful events. People dress in bright clothing and parade along the streets.

People in China are not encouraged to be religious, as it is goes against the ideals of communism. In the past, however, religion was an important part of Chinese life. The main religion was Buddhism, which is still followed by Tibetans. People also followed Taoism and the teachings of the philosopher, Confucius, who was born around 551 BC. Confucius believed that education, the family, and living together in peace and harmony were very important. Many Chinese people still follow his teachings today.

A monk from a Buddhist monastery in Xiahe. Buddhists believe that people are born over and over again. What they do in one life will have an effect on the next one. They can return to life as an animal, an insect or a human.

The Hanging Monastery at Datong. In rocky areas, buildings are sometimes built straight onto the cliffside.

Food and shopping

Chinese people love eating! It is an important part of our culture. Our meals can go on for a long time, especially when relatives are visiting! All the food is brought to the table at the same time in lots of little dishes. We use chopsticks to eat our food, instead of knives and forks. People usually drink tea with every meal, and beer is very popular.

Rice is the main ingredient in our cooking, but each region of China has its own special dishes. The food from Sichuan is hot and spicy. Beijing is famous for its crispy duck and steamed bread.

Vegetables are a major ingredient in Chinese cooking. They are usually stir-fried and served with thin strips of meat, and rice or noodles.

WEST ELEMENTARY
1322 CENTRAL
STOUGHTON,

Many people shop for their food in open-air markets. In country areas, families have small vegetable gardens beside their houses. Some villages even have their own fish ponds.

Cantonese cooking, which consists of dishes such as sweet and sour pork, and snacks known as *dim sum,* can be found in restaurants all over the world. Meat is very valuable. We have a recipe for every part of an animal, except for its fur or feathers! Some people like to eat sea slugs, jellyfish and duck tongues. My favorite treat is braised chicken's feet.

Chinese people use chopsticks to eat their food. But for some dishes a spoon is easier! Young children use spoons until they are old enough to handle chopsticks.

Make Yangzhou fried rice

This is called *Yangzhou chao fan* in Chinese.

Ask an adult to help you prepare this dish.

You will need:

- 500 grams (1 lb) long-grain rice
- large saucepan of water
- 2 tablespoons vegetable oil
- 2 eggs, beaten
- 6 spring onions, chopped
- a handful of chopped ham
- a handful of shrimp, peeled
- a handful of peas, cooked
- a handful of bean shoots
- 1 tablespoon soy sauce

What to do:

1 Cook the rice in the water for about 12 minutes. Drain with a sieve.

2 Heat a large wok. Pour in some of the vegetable oil. When the oil is hot, add the beaten eggs. Allow the eggs to set into a 'pancake', then flip the pancake over and cook the other side. Take the pancake out of the wok, roll it up and cut it into strips.

3 Add some more vegetable oil to the wok. Stir-fry the chopped spring onions for one minute.

4 Add the ham and shrimp. Stir-fry for two minutes.

5 Add the cooked peas. Stir-fry for one minute.

6 Add the cooked rice. Stir-fry for one minute.

7 Add the bean shoots, egg strips and soy sauce. Stir-fry everything for one minute.

8 Serve in small bowls. Use chopsticks to eat your fried rice!

Make a Chinese lantern

Make your own Chinese lantern for *Yuan Hsiao*, the Lantern Festival.

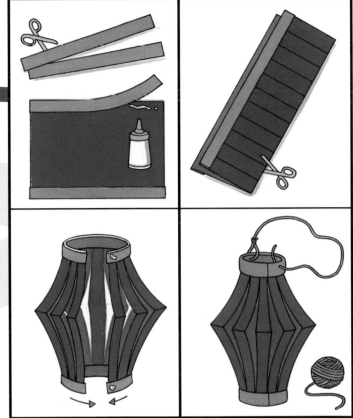

You will need:

- a sheet of gold or black paper
- a sheet of red paper
- pencil
- ruler
- glue or paste
- scissors
- string

What to do:

1 Cut two strips 3 cm-(1 in) wide from the long side of the gold or black paper.

2 Paste one strip to the top of the long side of the red paper. Paste the other strip to the bottom.

3 Fold the red paper in half along its length. Make a sharp crease.

4 Cut 10 slits into the red paper, starting from the folded edge of the red paper, and finishing at the pasted strips of gold or black paper. Unfold the paper.

5 Form the lantern by pasting the strips of gold or black paper together.

6 Punch two holes into one end of the lantern with the pencil.

7 Tie string through each hole to make a handle.

Hang your lantern inside your house. It will bring you good luck in the new year!

Landscape and climate

China is a land of many contrasts. In the west you will find the enormous, snow-capped mountains of the Himalayas. Mount Everest, on the border of Tibet and Nepal, is the highest mountain in the world. We call this mountain *Qomolangma*. Every couple of years it grows another centimeter (0.4 inch) in height as it continues to form.

The Plateau of Tibet is known as the 'roof of the world'. It is the largest high, flat area of land on Earth. The **plateau** is covered with patchy shrubs and grass. It is very cold in Tibet. There are only 50 days a year without frost.

In the north of China you will find the Gobi and Taklimakan deserts. These deserts are scorching hot in the daytime and freezing at night.

One-third of China is made up of mountains. Many of them are covered in snow all year.

The mountains around Yangshuo have been carved by the wind into interesting shapes.

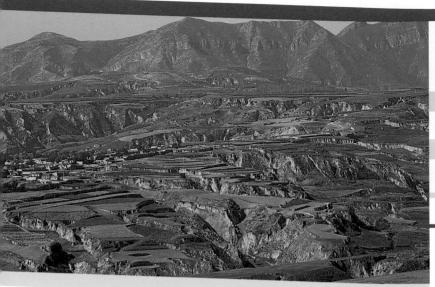

The Gobi Desert is made up of rock and gravel.

In the Taklimakan region, raindrops evaporate before they can touch the ground! It has fierce sandstorms that last for days.

In the south and east, the weather is much warmer and wetter. The land here is very good for farming. Most people live in the east of China, along the banks of the Yellow River, called *Huang He,* or the Yangtze River, called *Chang Jiang.* The Yellow River has overflowed more than 1,500 times in the past 3,000 years, destroying homes and crops. **Dikes** have been built along the banks to help control the floods.

The Yellow River has flooded many times, destroying homes and farms. It is known as 'China's sorrow'.

Plants and animals

China is home to many rare animals. In the northeast, you will find the Manchurian tiger, the red deer, the brown bear and the lynx. However, more and more people are moving into this area. As they cut down forests for farmland and build villages and roads, these animals are starting to die out. To help solve this problem, nature reserves are being built to protect **threatened wildlife**.

Although modern equipment is used for fishing these days, fishermen along the gentle rivers in the south of China still use cormorants to catch fish. Cormorants are large, glossy, black birds with big appetites. The fishermen train their birds to dive underwater, catch a fish, and bring it back up to them. The cormorants are allowed to eat every twelfth fish they catch. If the fisherman makes a mistake with the counting, his bird will squawk at him until it gets its dinner!

The giant panda is one of China's national treasures. Although people call them bears, pandas are more closely related to raccoons. Adult pandas weigh up to 100 kilograms (220 pounds). They eat huge amounts of bamboo, for up to 14 hours a day. Before people settled in China, pandas could be found living all over the country. But now there are less than 1,000 pandas left.

Bamboo is the only food that giant pandas will eat. It is mainly found in the forests of Sichuan province, in southwestern China. Bamboo grows very slowly. Some types can take up to 100 years to grow.

Cities and landmarks

China's cities are becoming bigger all the time, as more and more people move from the country to work in factories. The city streets are very crowded. Most people live in small apartments in tall buildings. Families often share kitchens and bathrooms with other families.

Population of major cities

Shanghai	14,190,000
Beijing	12,590,000
Tianjin	9,480,000
Chongqing	3,002,000

One of China's most important buildings, the Imperial Palace, is in the middle of Beijing. It was built for the Chinese royal family in the 1400s. The palace is also known as the Forbidden City, because ordinary people were not allowed inside. Now the palace, which has 9,999 rooms, has been turned into a museum. Anyone can visit it.

Tiantan, the Temple of Heaven, is one of the most beautiful buildings in Beijing. Many years ago Chinese emperors dressed in blue robes and prayed here for blessings for the people.

Beijing is our capital city. It used to be called Peking. It has a mix of old and new buildings. The old walls which once surrounded the city were knocked down in the 1950s because their narrow gates slowed down traffic. Shanghai, on the east coast, is not as big as Beijing, but it has more people. Shanghai is our main port. Its name means 'on the water'.

The Summer Palace in Beijing was a place of quiet retreat for the emperors of China. Its grounds contain a lake, a river, a mountain and a garden where people could reflect on the perfection and beauty of nature.

The Great Wall of China loops and slithers its way across our land like a giant snake. It is the biggest building in the world, and can even be seen from the moon! It stretches for thousands of miles all the way from Beijing to Inner Mongolia. Slaves and soldiers began building the wall about 2,300 years ago, to keep China's enemies out.

Industry and agriculture

Two-thirds of Chinese people live in the country, where most work as farmers. The main crops are rice, wheat, millet, maize, soybeans and sweet potatoes. Some farmers also produce cotton, peanuts, sugarcane, tea, silk cocoons and fruit, such as apples and mandarins.

Farm animals graze on the vast areas of grassland in Inner Mongolia and on the Qinghai–Tibet Plateau. Chinese farmers raise many different types of farm animals, including pigs, cattle, sheep, horses, camels, ducks and rabbits. Fish are caught in the rivers and sea.

For many years all business in China was controlled by the government. People were paid the same amount of money no matter how hard they worked. This was not good for the country.

Many farmers in China grow rice, especially in the Yangtze River valley in south China, and on the Yunnan–Guizhou Plateau.

In 1979, two new government plans allowed people to set up their own businesses. These ranged from selling flowers or mending shoes in the street, to factories making everything from noodles to bubble gum. Now China is a richer country.

Heavy industry in China is growing steadily. China now makes its own airplanes, ships, cars and satellites. It produces more steel than any other country in the world. Our two biggest exports are machinery and electronic products, such as computers and software. Other important industries include coal mining, textiles and clothing, processed food, and paper making. We also have factories that make household goods such as pottery, clocks, shoes and toys.

Not many farmers in China can afford modern equipment. Instead, they do most of the work by hand. These farmers are sifting wheat.

This woman runs her own shoe-mending business in the street.

Transportation

For thousands of years, the best way to travel, or move goods around, was by boat. The Chinese people built a huge system of **canals**, including the Grand Canal, which flows all the way from Beijing in the north to Hangzhou in the south. The southern part of the Grand Canal is still used today.

People travel on the rivers of China using many different kinds of boats. These include rafts, passenger boats, sailboats called junks, and floating homes called sampans.

There is now a good road system in China but not many people can afford to own cars, so most people travel to school or work by bicycle. For longer journeys, people travel by bus or train. China has 66,000 kilometers (41,000 miles) of railway tracks, more than any other Asian country. Trains are often very crowded. If you are travelling overnight, you can book a carriage with bunk beds, and buy tea and food on the train.

The bicycle is still the cheapest and most popular form of transportation in China.

The streets of Shanghai are crowded with buses, cars, bicycles, motorbikes and pedestrians.

History and government

Ancient China

China is a very old **civilization**. A skull was found in a cave near Beijing which showed that people have been living in this country for more than 600,000 years!

For many centuries, China was ruled by powerful royal families known as **dynasties**. In 221 BC a tyrannical emperor named Qin Shihuang united all the different areas of China. Although he was only 13 when he became emperor, he treated his opponents cruelly. If any of his scholars disagreed with him, or seemed smarter than him, he had them burned alive. After Qin was overthrown, other dynasties came to power. The two most important of these were the Han dynasty and the Tang dynasty.

Mao Zedong, the head of the Chinese Communist Party, was the leader of China from 1949 to 1976. He tried to improve the lives of poor people by arranging things so that 'everything belonged to everybody'. This was called the Cultural Revolution. However, this revolution also destroyed many great buildings and priceless treasures, and ruined the lives of many people.

Tiananmen Square, in central Beijing, was where thousands of students gathered to protest in 1989. They decided that the government had too much control over people's lives. Many of the students were killed by government troops.

Modern China

In 1911, the final dynasty, the Qing dynasty, was overthrown by the people. China became a republic in 1912. Since then, China has had several leaders. The Nationalist Party was led by Chiang Kai Shek. Mao Zedong took over in 1949, when the Communists defeated the **Nationalists**. After Deng Xiaoping came to power in 1977, China became a more open place, and life began to get better.

Although Hong Kong and Macao were once ruled by other countries (Britain and Portugal), they have now been returned to China. This is Hong Kong today.

Fact file

		Population	Land area
Official name People's Republic of China		1,247,000,000 people in 1998. 30 percent live in urban areas, 70 percent live in rural areas	9,600,000 square kilometers (3.7 million square miles)
Government communist republic	**Languages** Putonghua (Mandarin, the official language), Yue (Cantonese), Tibetan, Wu, Xiang, Uyghur and many other local languages		**Religions** Confucianism, Buddhism, Taoism, Islam, Christianity
Currency Renminbi (RMB). The basic unit is the yuan		**Capital city** Beijing	**Major cities** Shanghai, Guangzhou, Nanjing, Tianjin, Shenyang, Wuhan, Chengdu
	Number of islands 5,400	**Climate** Wide-ranging: from tropical in the south, to subarctic in the north, to desert in the west	
Major rivers *Chang Jiang* (Yangtze), *Huang He* (Yellow)			**Highest mountain** Mt Qomolangma (Mt. Everest), 8,848 meters (29,030 feet)
Main farm products grains, cotton, nuts, sugarcane, tea, tobacco, silk cocoons, fruit, pork, chickens	**Main industries** iron, steel, coal, oil, machine building, electronics, aircraft and spacecraft, satellites, textiles, cement, household goods		**Natural resources** coal, iron ore, tin, tungsten, antimony, zinc, lead, mercury

Glossary

calligraphy	artistic handwriting done with a brush and ink
canal	a waterway that has been dug across land
civilization	the way of life of a particular people or nation
communism	the political idea that everything should be owned and controlled by the community and shared between the people
dike	a wall or dam built to hold back water
dynasty	a series of rulers who are from the same family
gongu/**kung fu**	a Chinese martial art or form of karate
industrialized	describes a country which uses machinery in making products and in farming
mah jong	a Chinese game played with small tiles
minority group	a group of people who are of a different race, nationality or religion from a larger group living in the same area
Nationalists	people who support their nation ruling itself independently
plateau	a large, flat area of land that is higher than the land around it
province	a large division or part of a country
rice paddy	a field used for growing rice
tai ji quan/ *tai chi*	a Chinese martial art consisting of graceful movements
threatened wildlife	animals or plants likely to become endangered species unless steps are taken to protect them

Index